THE UKULELE
3 Chord Songbook

PLAY 50 GREAT SONGS WITH JUST 3 EASY CHORDS!

T0066593

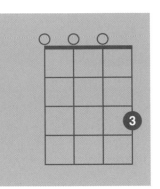 

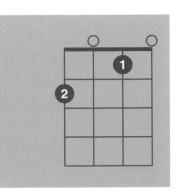 

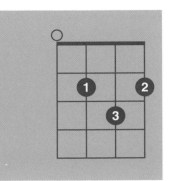 

ISBN 978-1-4950-0914-3

HAL•LEONARD®
CORPORATION
7777 W. BLUEMOUND RD. P.O. BOX 13819 MILWAUKEE, WI 53213

Visit Hal Leonard Online at
www.halleonard.com

3 Chord Songbook

PLAY 50 GREAT SONGS WITH JUST 3 EASY CHORDS!

Contents

Ain't That a Shame

Words and Music by Antoine Domino and Dave Bartholomew

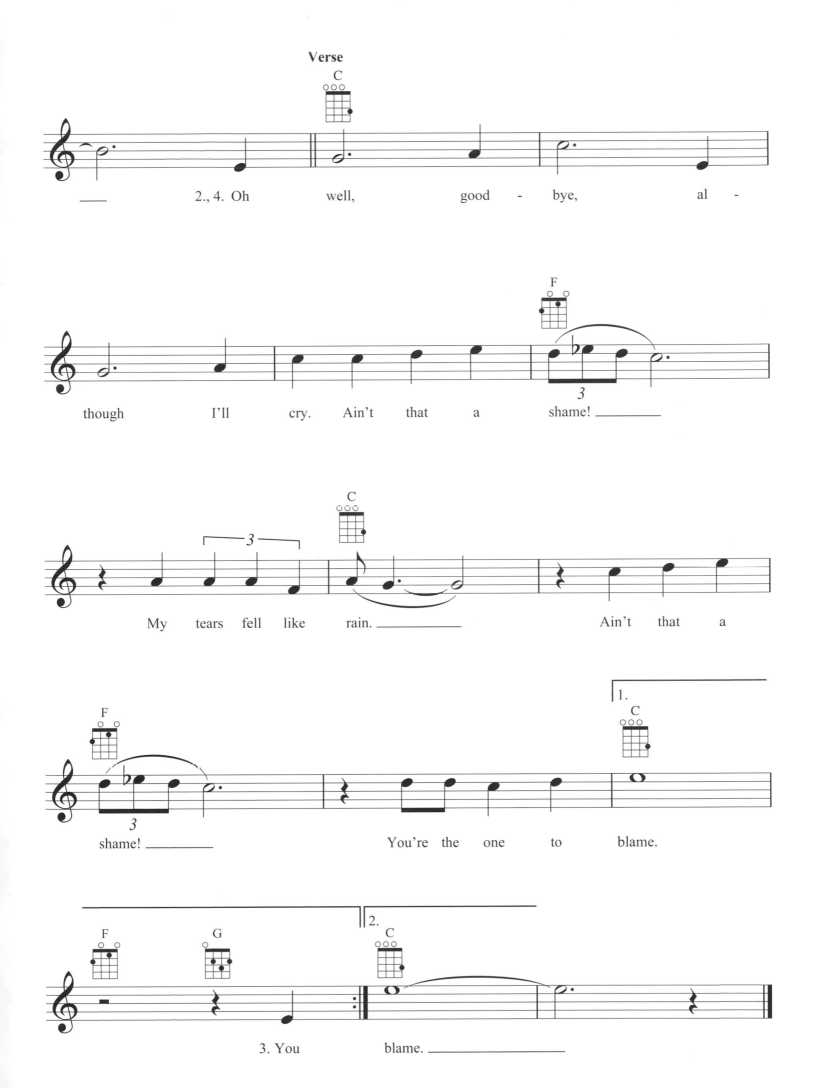

Verse

2., 4. Oh well, good - bye, al -

though I'll cry. Ain't that a shame! _____

My tears fell like rain. _____ Ain't that a

1.

shame! _____ You're the one to blame.

2.

3. You blame. _____

All Apologies

Words and Music by Kurt Cobain

(Instrumental)

1. What else should I be? _____   All a - pol - o - gies. _
2. *See additional lyrics*

_____   What else could I say? _____

Ev - 'ry - one _____ was gay. _____   What else could I write? _

I don't have __ the right. __

What else should I be? _____ All a-pol - o-gies. __

Chorus

In the sun, _____ in the sun _____ I feel __ as one. __

__ In the sun, _____ in the sun _____ I'm

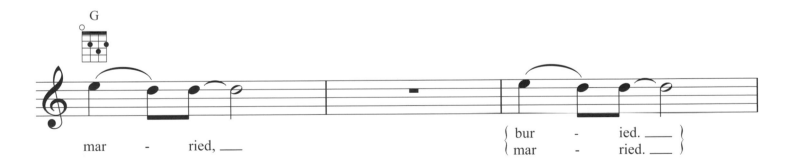

mar - ried, __ { bur - ied. __ }
{ mar - ried. __ }

Mar - ried, __

Interlude
C

bur - ied. ___ Yeah, yeah, yeah, yeah. ___

(Instrumental)

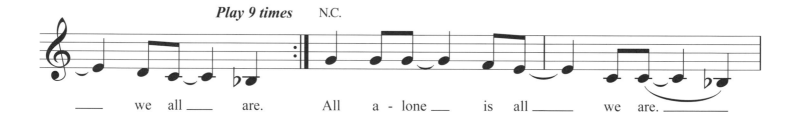

Outro
C

All a - lone ___ is all ___ we all ___ are. All a - lone ___ is all ___

Play 9 times   N.C.

___ we all ___ are. All a - lone ___ is all ___ we are. ___

All a - lone ___ is all ___ we are. ___

Additional Lyrics

2. I wish I was like you, easily amused.
Find my nest of salt. Everything is my fault.
I'll take all the blame, aqua seafoam shame.
Sunburn with freezer burn. Choking on the ashes of her enemy.

Authority Song

Words and Music by John Mellencamp

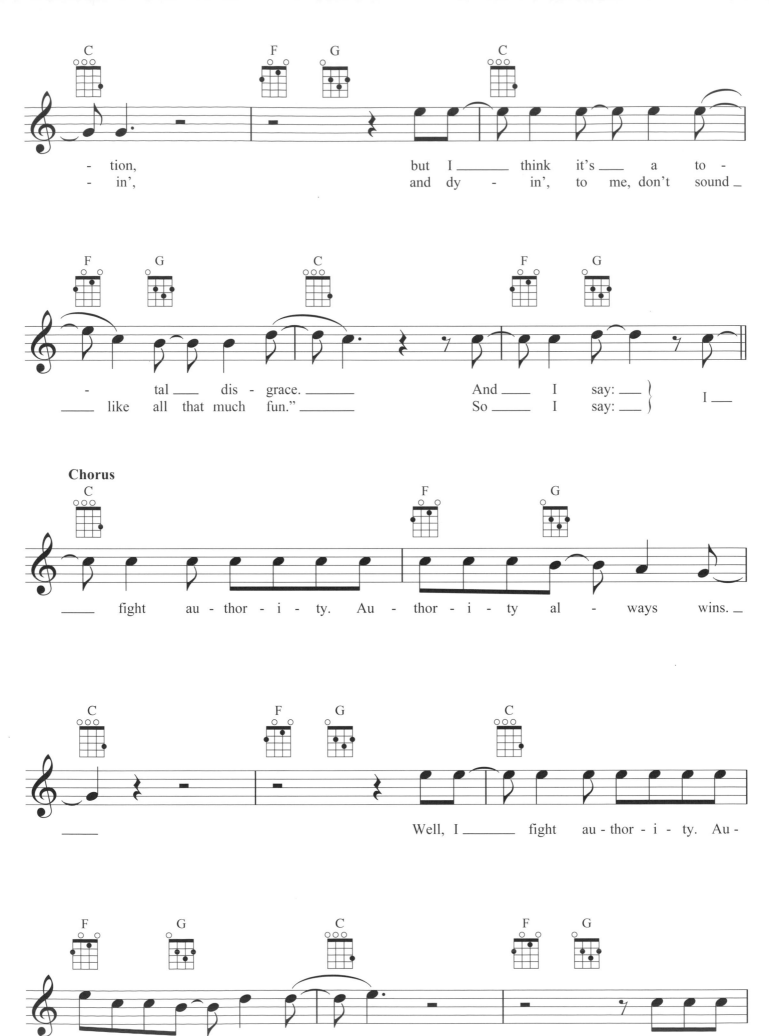

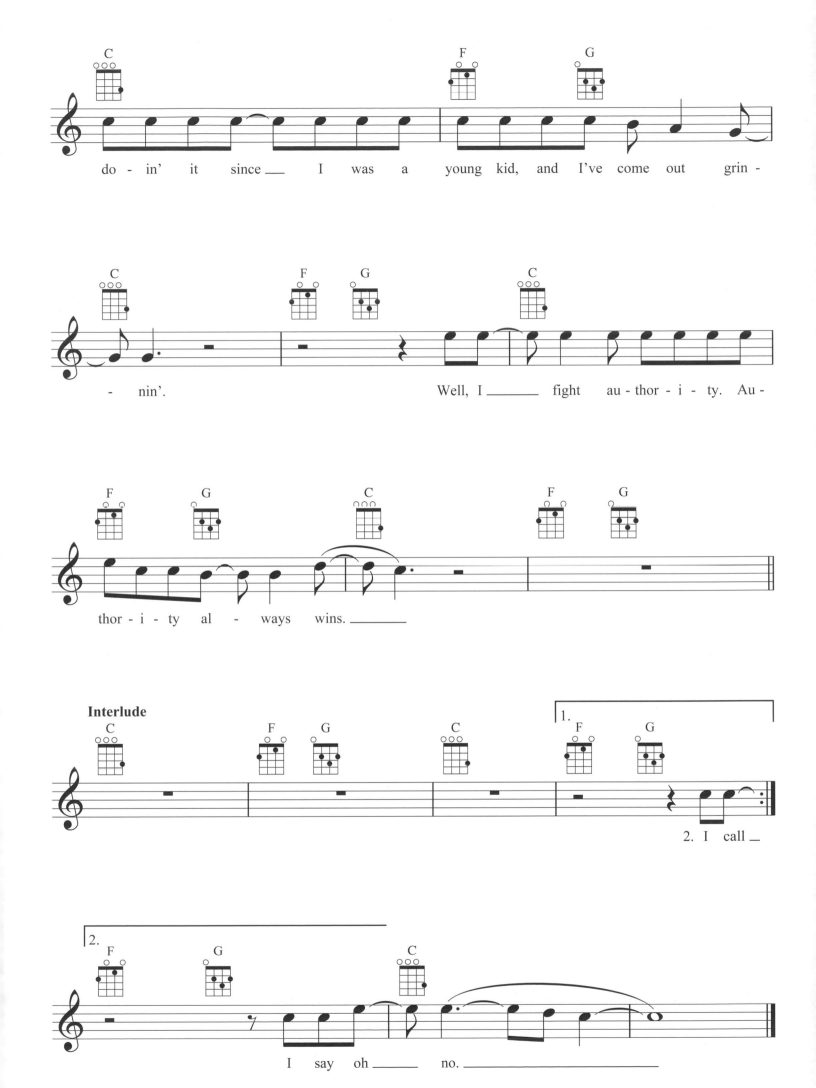

At the Hop

Words and Music by Arthur Singer, John Madara and David White

sweep - in' the na - tion at the hop.
get _____ their kicks _____ at the hop.

Chorus

Let's go to the hop! (Oh, ba - by.)

Let's go to the hop! (Oh, ba - by.) Let's go to the hop!

(Oh, ba - by.) Let's go to the hop! (Oh, ba - by.)

1.

Come on, let's go to the hop!

2.

2. Well, you can let's go to the hop!

Bad Moon Rising

Words and Music by John Fogerty

1. I see a bad _____ moon _____ ris -
2., 3. *See additional lyrics*

- in'. I see

trou - ble on the way. _____

I see earth - quakes and light - nin'.

Additional Lyrics

2. I hear hurricanes a-blowin'.
   I know the end is comin' soon.
   I fear rivers overflowin'.
   I hear the voice of rage and ruin.

3. Hope you got your things together.
   Hope you are quite prepared to die.
   Looks like we're in for nasty weather.
   One eye is taken for an eye.

The Ballad of John and Yoko

Words and Music by John Lennon and Paul McCartney

First note

Verse
Moderate Rock

1. Stand - ing in the dock at South - amp - ton,
2. Fi - n'lly made the plane in - to Par - is,
(3.) Par - is to the Am - ster - dam Hil - ton,

tryin' to get to Hol - land or France. ____ The
hon - ey - moon - ing down by the Seine. ____ Pe - ter
talk - ing in our beds for a week. ____ The

man in the mac ____ said, ____ "You've got to go back." ____ You know they
Brown called to say, ____ "You can make it O - K. ____ You can get
news - peo - ple said, ____ "Say, what're you do - ing in bed?" ____ I said, "We're

did - n't e - ven give us a chance. ____ }
mar - ried in Gi - bral - tar, near Spain." ____ } Christ! You know it ain't eas -
on - ly tryin' to get us some peace." ____ }

Chorus

- y, _____ you know how hard it can be. _____

The way things are go - ing, ___ they're gon - na cru - ci - fy ___

me. *(Instrumental)*

1., 2.

2. _____
3. Drove _ from

3.

Bridge

Sav - ing up your mon - ey for a rain - y day, ___ giv - ing all your clothes to char - i -

ty. Last night the wife said, "Oh boy, when you're dead, you

don't take noth-ing with you but your soul." _____ Think!

Verse
C

4. Made a light-ning trip to Vi - en - na,
5. Caught the ear - ly plane back to Lon - don,

eat-ing choc -'late cake in a bag. ___ The news-pa-pers said, _____ "She's
fif - ty a-corns tied in a sack. ___ The men from the press __ said, _ "We

gone to his head; _____ they look just like two gu-rus in drag." _
wish you suc-cess; _____ it's good to have the both of you back." _

Chorus
F

___ } Christ! You know it ain't eas - y, you know how hard it can be. _

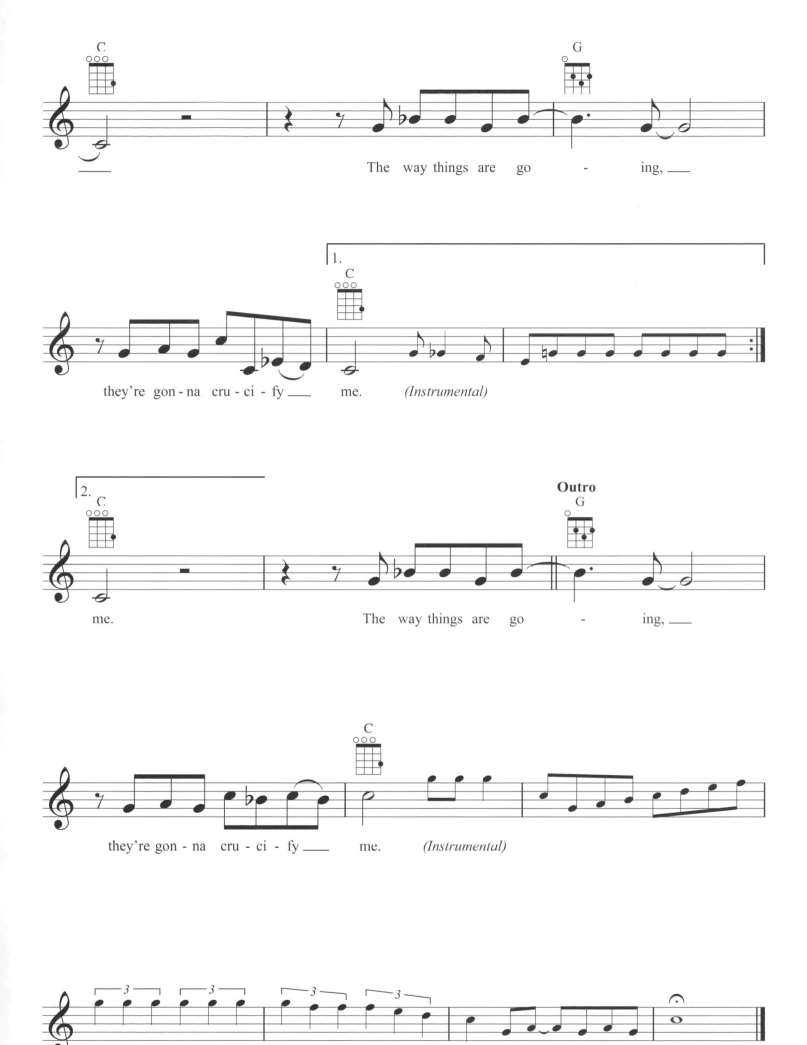

The way things are go - ing, ___

1.

they're gon - na cru - ci - fy ___ me. *(Instrumental)*

2.

me. The way things are go - ing, ___

Outro

they're gon - na cru - ci - fy ___ me. *(Instrumental)*

Be-Bop-A-Lula

Words and Music by Tex Davis and Gene Vincent

First note

Be - bop - a - lu - la, she's my ba - by.

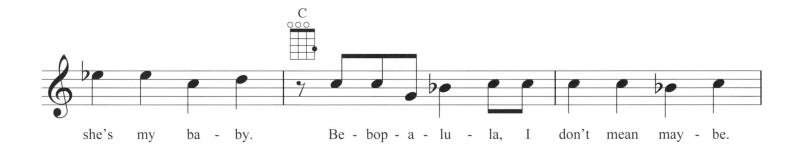

Be - bop - a - lu - la, I don't mean may - be. Be - bop - a - lu - la,

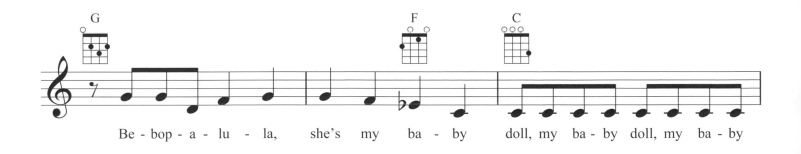

she's my ba - by. Be - bop - a - lu - la, I don't mean may - be.

Be - bop - a - lu - la, she's my ba - by doll, my ba - by doll, my ba - by

Blowin' in the Wind

Words and Music by Bob Dylan

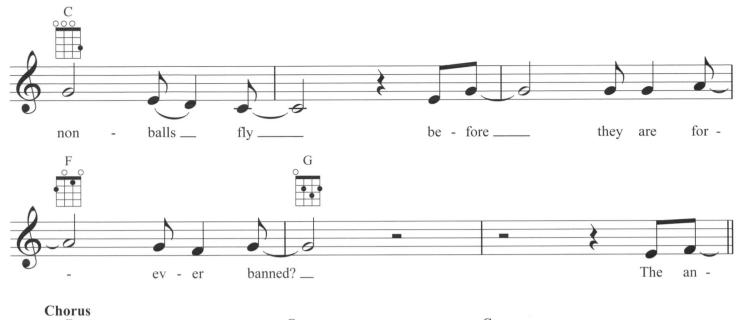

non - balls ___ fly ___ be - fore ___ they are for -

- ev - er banned? ___ The an -

Chorus

- swer, my friend, ___ is blow - in' in ___ the wind. ___

The an - swer is blow - in' in ___ the wind. ___

1., 2.   3.

Additional Lyrics

2. How many years can a mountain exist
    Before it is washed to the sea?
    How many years can some people exist
    Before they're allowed to be free?
    Yes, and how many times can a man turn his head
    And pretend that he just doesn't see?

3. How many times must a man look up
    Before he can see the sky?
    How many ears must one man have
    Before he can hear people cry?
    Yes, and how many deaths will it take till he knows
    That too many people have died?

Boot Scootin' Boogie

Words and Music by Ronnie Dunn

Additional Lyrics

2. I got a good job, I work hard for my money.
   When it's quittin' time, I hit the door runnin'.
   I fire up my pickup truck and let the horses run.
   I go flyin' down that highway to that hideaway
   Stuck out in the woods, to do the boot scootin' boogie.

3. The bartender asks me, "Say, son, what'll it be?"
   I want a shot at that redhead yonder lookin' at me.
   The dance floor's hoppin' and it's hotter than the Fourth of July.
   I see outlaws, in-laws, crooks and straights,
   All out makin' it shake, doin' the boot scootin' boogie.

Bread and Butter

Words and Music by Larry Parks and Jay Turnbow

Verse
Moderately, in 2

1. I like bread and but - ter, I like toast and jam.
2., 3. *See additional lyrics*

That's what my ba - by feeds __ me; I'm her lov - in' man.

Chorus

(1., 2.) He likes bread and but - ter, he likes toast and jam. That's what his ba - by
(3.) *See additional lyrics*

1., 2. | **3.**

feeds him; he's her lov - in' man. with some oth - er man. _____

Additional Lyrics

2. She don't cook mashed potatoes,
   She don't cook T-bone steak,
   She don't feed me peanut butter.
   She knows that I can't take.

3. I got home early one mornin'.
   Much to my surprise,
   She was eatin' chicken and dumplins
   With some other guy.

   Chorus: No more bread and butter,
   No more toast and jam.
   He found his baby eatin'
   With some other man.

A Boy Named Sue

Words and Music by Shel Silverstein

First note

Moderately bright

Verse

(Spoken:) 1. Well, my daddy left home when I was three and he didn't leave much to

3., 5., 7., 9. *See additional lyrics*

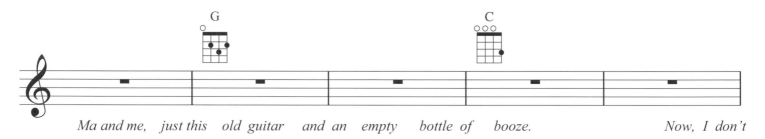

Ma and me, just this old guitar and an empty bottle of booze. Now, I don't

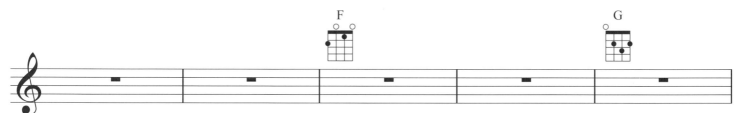

blame him because he run and hid, but the meanest thing that he ever did was, before he left he

Verse

went and named me Sue. 2. Well, he must have thought it was

4., 6., 8., 10. *See additional lyrics*

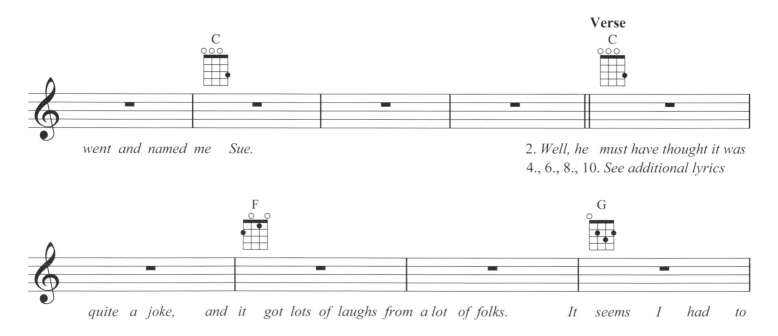

quite a joke, and it got lots of laughs from a lot of folks. It seems I had to

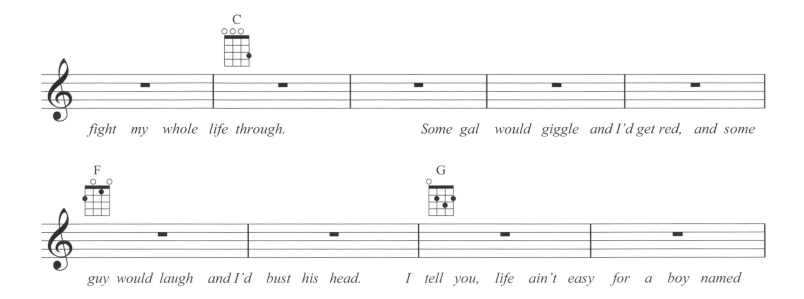

fight   my   whole   life   through.   *Some   gal   would   giggle   and   I'd   get   red,   and   some*

guy   would   laugh   and   I'd   bust   his   head.   *I   tell   you,   life   ain't   easy   for   a   boy   named*

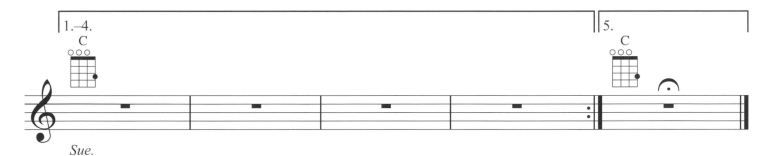

Sue.

Additional Lyrics

3. *Well, I grew up quick and I grew up mean;*
   My fists got hard and my wits got keen.
   Roamed from town to town to hide my shame.
   But I made me a vow to the moon and stars,
   I'd search the honky-tonks and bars,
   And kill that man that give me that awful name.

4. *Well, it was Gatlinburg in mid July,*
   And I had just hit town and my throat was dry.
   I'd thought I'd stop and have myself a brew.
   At an old saloon on a street of mud,
   There at a table dealin' stud,
   Sat the dirty, mangy dog that named me Sue.

5. *Well, I knew that snake was my own sweet dad*
   From a worn-out picture that my mother had.
   And I knew that scar on his cheek and his evil eye.
   He was big and bent and gray and old,
   And I looked at him and my blood ran cold,
   And I said, "My name is Sue. How do you do?
   Now you gonna die." Yeah, that's what I told him.

6. *Well, I hit him hard right between the eyes,*
   And he went down, but to my surprise
   He come up with a knife and cut off a piece of my ear.
   But I busted a chair right across his teeth
   And we crashed through the wall and into the street,
   Kickin' and a-gougin' in the mud and the blood and the beer.

7. *I tell you, I've fought tougher men,*
   But I really can't remember when.
   He kicked like a mule and he bit like a crocodile.
   I heard him laugh and then I heard him cussin'.
   He went for his gun and I pulled mine first.
   He stood there lookin' at me and I saw him smile.

8. *And he said, "Son, this world is rough,*
   And if a man's gonna make it, he's gotta be tough.
   And I know I wouldn't be there to help you along.
   So I gave you that name and I said goodbye.
   I knew you'd have to get tough or die.
   And it's that name that helped to make you strong.

9. *Yeah, he said, "Now, you just fought one helluva fight,*
   And I know you hate me and you've got the right
   To kill me now, and I wouldn't blame you if you do.
   But you ought to thank me before I die
   For the gravel in your guts and the spit in your eye,
   'Cause I'm the son of a bitch that named you Sue."
   Yeah, what could I do? What could I do?

10. *I got all choked up and I threw down my gun,*
    Called him my pa and he called me his son.
    And I come away with a different point of view.
    And I think about him now and then,
    Ev'ry time I try and ev'ry time I win.
    And if I ever have a son, I think I'm gonna name him...
    Bill or George. Anything but Sue.
    I still hate that man. Yeah.

Deportee

(Plane Wreck at Los Gatos)

Words by Woody Guthrie
Music by Martin Hoffman

1. The crops are all in and the peach-es are rot-t'ning,

(2.–6.) *See additional lyrics*

the or-an-ges piled in their cre-o-sote dumps.

You're fly-ing 'em back to the Mex-i-can bor-der, to

pay all their mon-ey to wade back a-gain. _____ Good-

bye to my Juan, ___ good-bye, Ro-sa-li-ta. A-diós, mis a-

mi - gos,   Je - sús   y   Ma - ri - a. _____   You   won't   have   your

names   when   you   ride   the   big   air - plane;   all   they   will

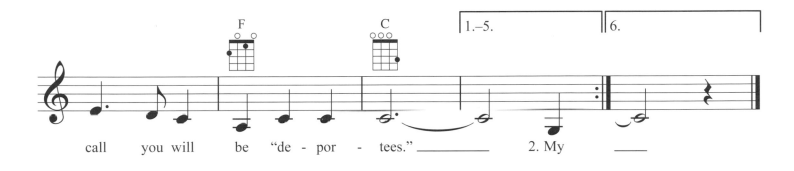

call   you   will   be   "de - por - tees." _____   2. My _____

Additional Lyrics

2. My father's own father, he waded that river;
   They took all the money he made in his life.
   My brothers and sisters come working the fruit trees,
   And they rode the truck till they took down and died.

3. Some of us are illegal and some are not wanted;
   Our work contract's out and we have to move on.
   Six hundred miles to that Mexican border;
   They chase us like outlaws, like rustlers, like thieves.

4. We died in your hills and we died in your deserts.
   We died in your valleys and died on your plains.
   We died 'neath your trees and we died in your bushes.
   Both sides of the river, we died just the same.

5. The sky plane caught fire over Los Gatos Canyon,
   A fireball of lightning, and shook all our hills.
   Who are all these friends, all scattered like dry leaves?
   The radio says they are just deportees.

6. Is this the best way we can grow our big orchards?
   Is this the best way we can grow our good fruit?
   To fall like dry leaves to rot on my topsoil
   And be called by no name except "Deportees"?

Donna

Words and Music by Ritchie Valens

Down on the Corner

Words and Music by John Fogerty

First note

Verse
Brightly, in 2

1. Ear - ly in the eve - nin', just a - bout sup-per - time, __
2., 3. *See additional lyrics*

__ o - ver by the court - house they're

start - ing to un - wind. __ Four kids on the cor - ner

tryin' to bring you up. __ Wil - ly picks a tune __

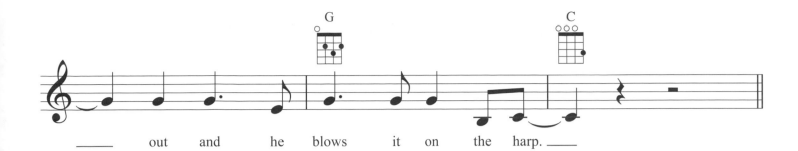

_____ out and he blows it on the harp. _____

Chorus

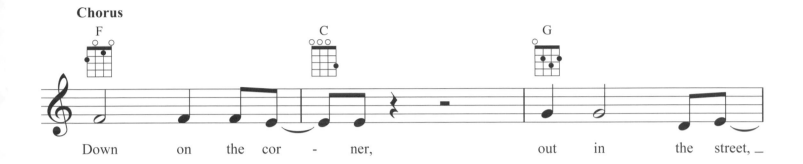

Down on the cor - ner, out in the street, _

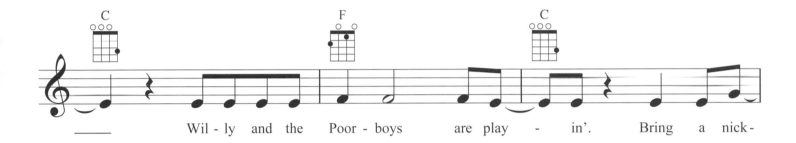

_____ Wil - ly and the Poor - boys are play - in'. Bring a nick-

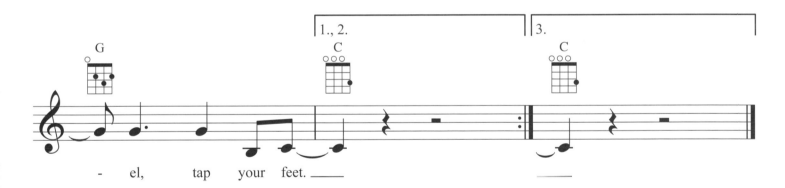

- el, tap your feet. _____

Additional Lyrics

2. Rooster hits the washboard and people just gotta smile.
   Blinky thumps the gut bass and solos for a while.
   Poorboy twangs the rhythm out on his kalamazoo.
   Willy goes into a dance and doubles on kazoo.

3. You don't need a penny just to hang around,
   But if you've got a nickel, won't you lay your money down?
   Over on the corner there's a happy noise.
   People come from all around to watch the magic boy.

For What It's Worth

Words and Music by Stephen Stills

1. There's some-thing hap-pen-ing here, _____ but what it
2.– 4. *See additional lyrics*

is ain't ex-act-ly clear. _____ There's a

man with a gun o-ver there _____ tell-ing

me I've got to be-ware. _____ I think it's time we

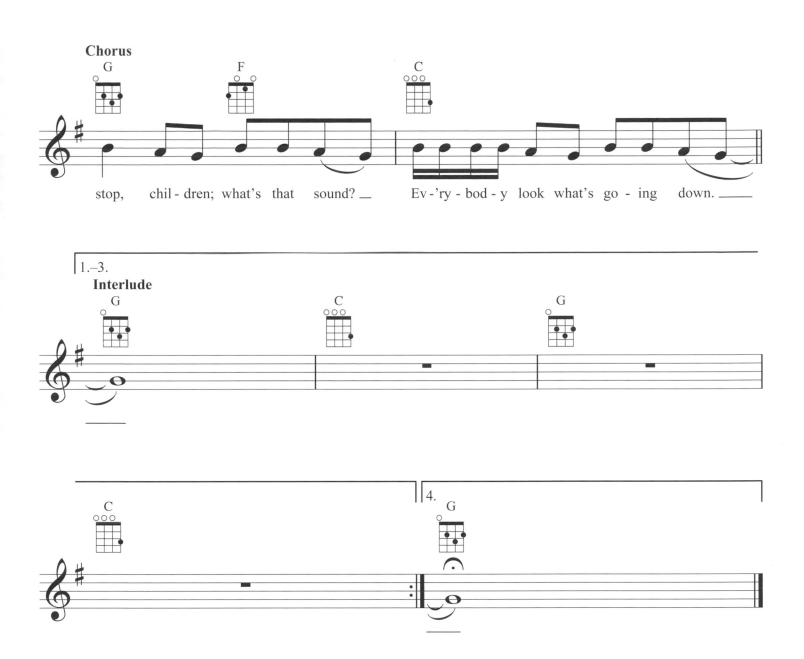

Chorus

stop, chil - dren; what's that sound? __ Ev - 'ry - bod - y look what's go - ing down. _____

1.–3.
Interlude

4.

Additional Lyrics

2. There's battle lines being drawn.
   Nobody's right if everybody's wrong.
   Young people speaking their minds,
   Getting so much resistance from behind.
Chorus: I think it's time we stop; hey, what's that sound?
   Ev'rybody look what's going down.

3. What a field day for the heat.
   A thousand people in the street
   Singing songs and carrying signs,
   Mostly say, "Hooray for our side."
Chorus: It's time we stop; hey, what's that sound?
   Ev'rybody look what's going down.

4. Paranoia strikes deep.
   Into your life it will creep.
   It starts when you're always afraid.
   You step out of line, the man come and take you away.
Chorus: We better stop; hey, what's that sound?
   Ev'rybody look what's going down.

Honeycomb

Words and Music by Bob Merrill

Outro-Chorus

Hound Dog

Words and Music by Jerry Leiber and Mike Stoller

I Love Rock 'n Roll

Words and Music by Alan Merrill and Jake Hooker

2.

Pre-Chorus

I said, "Can I take you home ___ where we can be a-lone?"

Next, we were mov-in' on, ___ and he was with me, yeah, me.

And we'll be mov-in' on ___ and sing-in' that same old song, yeah, with me, ___ sing-in': I love

Outro-Chorus

rock 'n' roll. So put an-oth-er dime in the juke-box, ba-by. I love

rock 'n' roll. So come and take your time and dance with me.

Free Fallin'

Words and Music by Tom Petty and Jeff Lynne

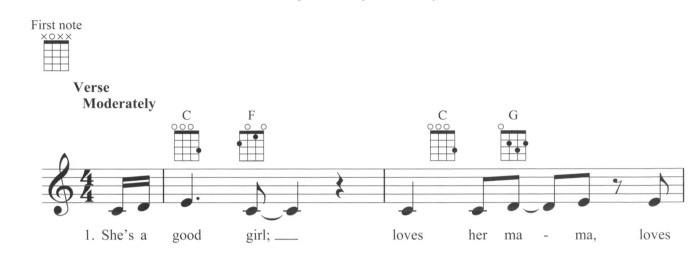

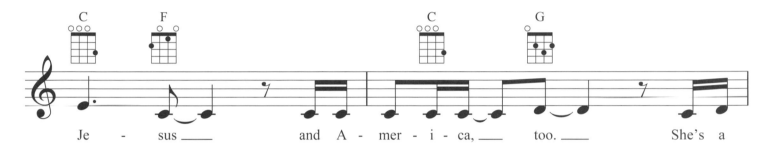

1. She's a good girl; ___ loves her ma - ma, loves

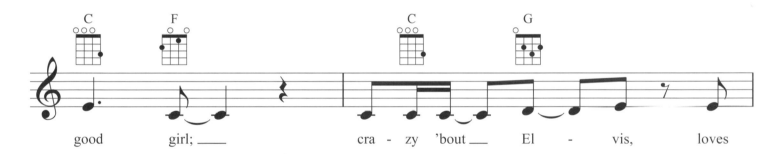

Je - sus ___ and A - mer - i - ca, ___ too. ___ She's a

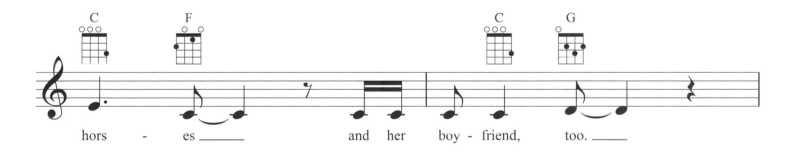

good girl; ___ cra - zy 'bout ___ El - vis, loves

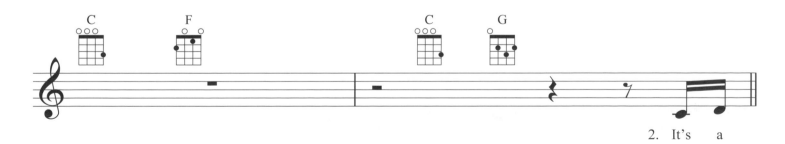

hors - es ___ and her boy - friend, too. ___

2. It's a

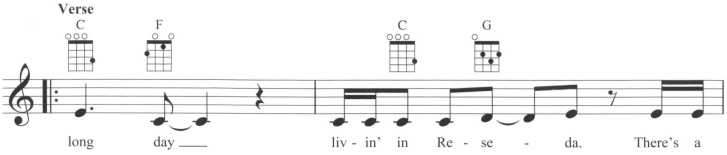

Verse

long day ____ liv - in' in Re - se - da. There's a

(3., 4.) *See additional lyrics*

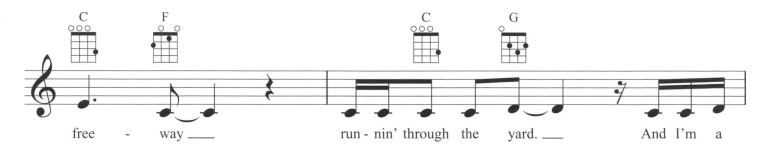

free - way ____ run - nin' through the yard. ____ And I'm a

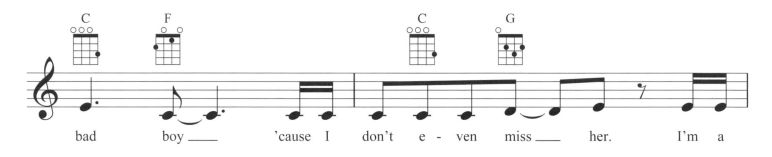

bad boy ____ 'cause I don't e - ven miss ____ her. I'm a

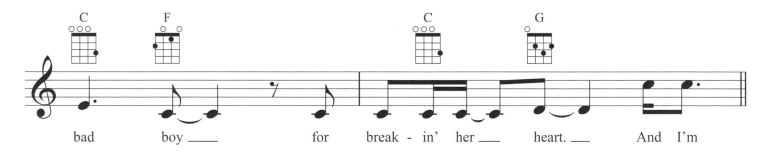

bad boy ____ for break - in' her ____ heart. ____ And I'm

Chorus

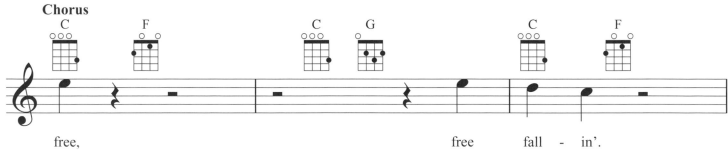

free, free fall - in'.

Yeah, I'm free, free

Additional Lyrics

3. All the vampires walkin' through the valley
   Move west down Ventura Boulevard.
   And all the bad boys are standing in the shadows,
   And the good girls are home with broken hearts.

4. Wanna glide down over Mulholland.
   I wanna write her name in the sky.
   I wanna free fall out into nothin'.
   Gonna leave this world for a while.

I Still Haven't Found What I'm Looking For

Words and Music by U2

1. I have climbed _ high-est moun-tain, I have
(2., 3.) *See additional lyrics*

run _ through the fields on-ly to be with _ you, _

_ on-ly to be with _ you. _ I have

run, _ I have crawled, I have scaled _ these cit-

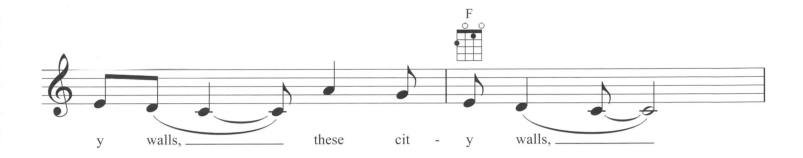

y   walls, _____ these cit - y   walls, _____

on - ly to   be   with ___ you. _____   But I still ___

Chorus

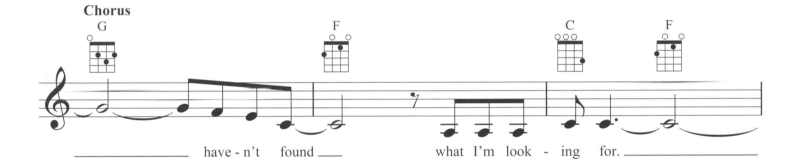

_____ have - n't found ___   what I'm look - ing for. _____

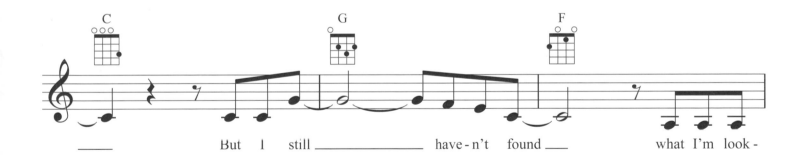

___   But I   still _____ have - n't found ___   what I'm look -

ing for. _____   2. I   have ___   But I still ___
                                 3. I   be -

Outro-Chorus

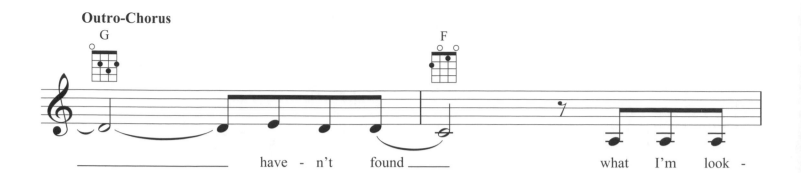

have - n't found _____ what I'm look -

ing for. _____ But I still _____ have - n't found _

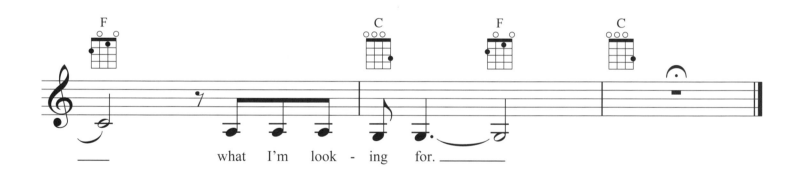

_____ what I'm look - ing for. _____

Additional Lyrics

2. I have kissed honey lips, felt the healing fingertips.
   It burned like fire, this burning desire.
   I have spoke with the tongue of angels, I have held the hand of the devil.
   It was warm in the night, I was cold as a stone.

3. I believe in the kingdom come, then all the colors will bleed into one,
   Bleed into one. But, yes, I'm still runnin'.
   You broke the bonds and you loosed the chains, carried the cross of my shame,
   Of my shame. You know I believe it.

Leaving on a Jet Plane

Words and Music by John Denver

Chorus

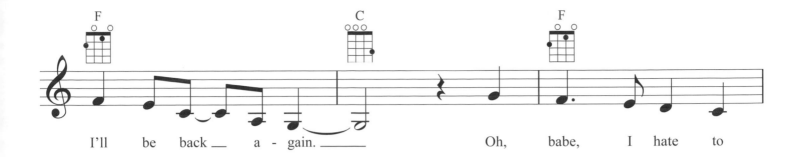

I'll be back __ a - gain. _____ Oh, babe, I hate to

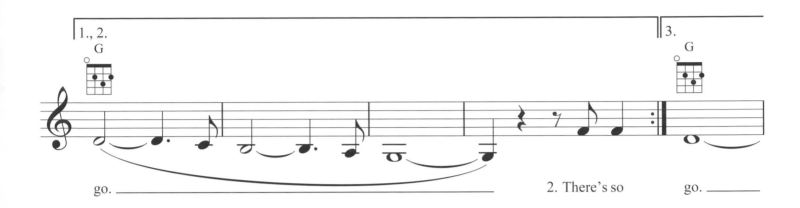

1., 2.
G

go. _____ 2. There's so go. _____

3.
G

Outro

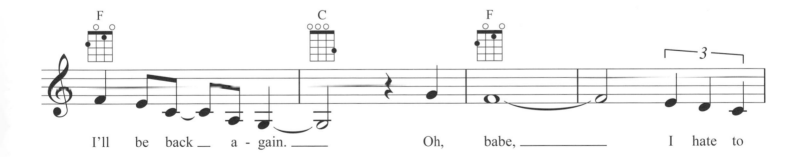

__ I'm leav - in' on a jet __ plane, don't know when

I'll be back __ a - gain. _____ Oh, babe, _____ I hate to

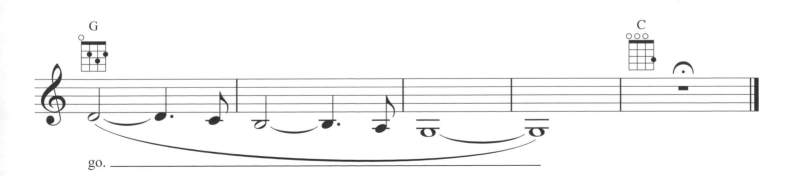

go. _____

I've Got a Tiger by the Tail

Words and Music by Buck Owens and Harlan Howard

just the kind ___ to fit my dreams and plans. ___

Now the pace ___ we're liv-ing takes the wind from my sails, ___

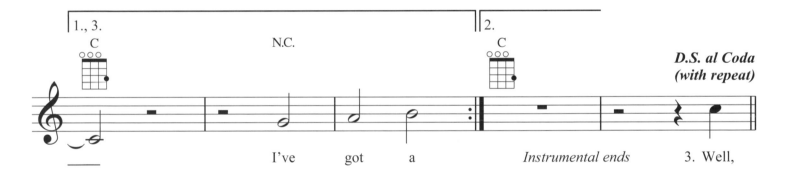

___ and it looks like I've got a ti - ger by the tail. ___

1., 3. ___ N.C. I've got a

2. *Instrumental ends* 3. Well,

D.S. al Coda
(with repeat)

Coda

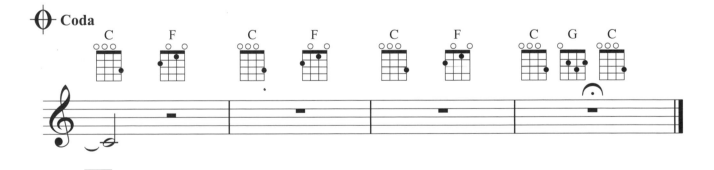

___

Additional Lyrics

3. Well, ev'ry night you drag me where the bright lights are found.
   There ain't no way to slow you down.
   I'm about as helpless as a leaf in a gale,
   And it looks like I've got a tiger by the tail.

Jealous Heart

Words and Music by Jenny Lou Carson

1. Jeal - ous heart, oh, jeal - ous heart stop beat - ing.
(2.) filled my con - science full of sor - row,
(3.) heart, why did I let you rule me,

Can't you see the dam - age you have
for I know she nev - er was un -
when I knew the end would bring me

done? You have driv - en her a - way for -
true. Jeal - ous heart, why did you make her
pain? Now she's gone, she's gone and found an -

ev - er. Jeal - ous heart, now I'm the lone - ly
hate me? Now there's noth - ing left but jeal - ous
oth - er. Oh, I'll nev - er see my love a -

King of the Road

Words and Music by Roger Miller

Little Honda

Words and Music by Brian Wilson and Mike Love

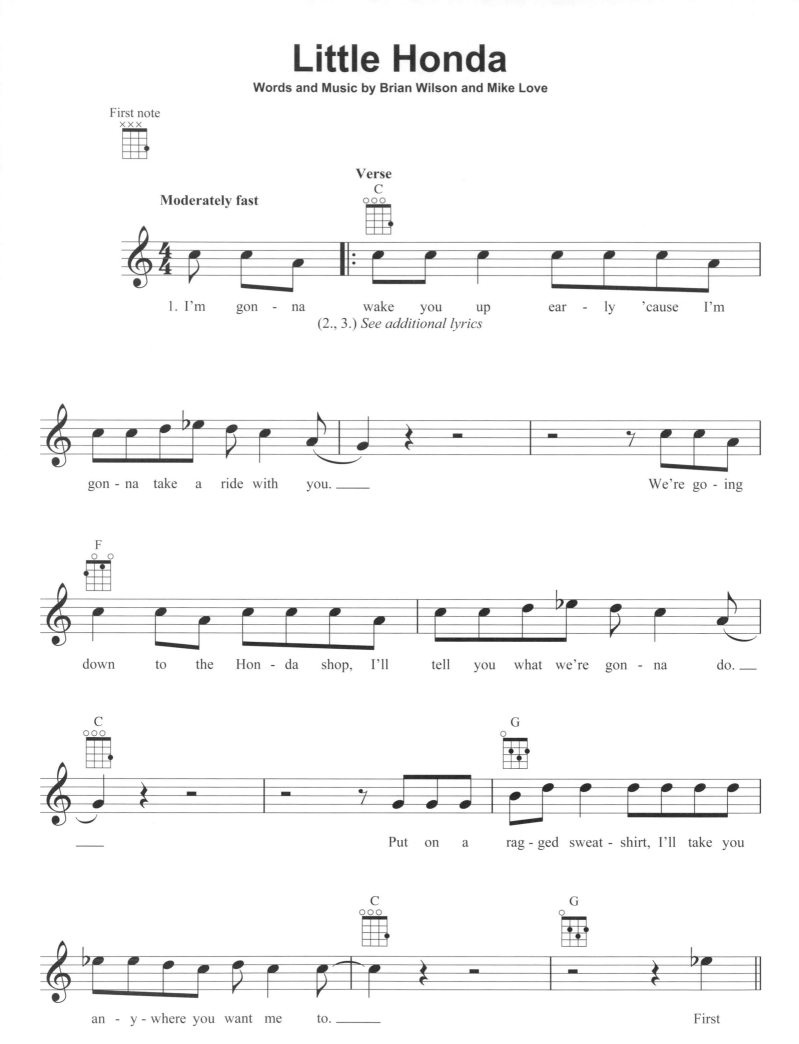

First note

Moderately fast

Verse

1. I'm gon - na wake you up ear - ly 'cause I'm

(2., 3.) *See additional lyrics*

gon - na take a ride with you. ___ We're go - ing

down to the Hon - da shop, I'll tell you what we're gon - na do. ___

___ Put on a rag - ged sweat - shirt, I'll take you

an - y - where you want me to. ___ First

Additional Lyrics

2. It's not a big motorcycle, just a groovy little motor bike.
   It's more fun than a barrel of monkeys, that two-wheeled bike.
   We'll ride on out of the town to anyplace I know you like.

3. It climbs the hills like a Matchless 'cause my Honda's built really light.
   When I go into the turns, tilt with me and hang on tight.
   I'd better turn on the lights so we can ride my Honda tonight.

Move It On Over

Words and Music by Hank Williams

No Particular Place to Go

Words and Music by Chuck Berry

1. Rid-ing a-long in my au-to-mo-bile, my ba-by be-side me at the wheel.

(2.–4.) *See additional lyrics*

I stole a kiss at the turn of a mile, my cu-ri-os-i-ty run-ning wild.

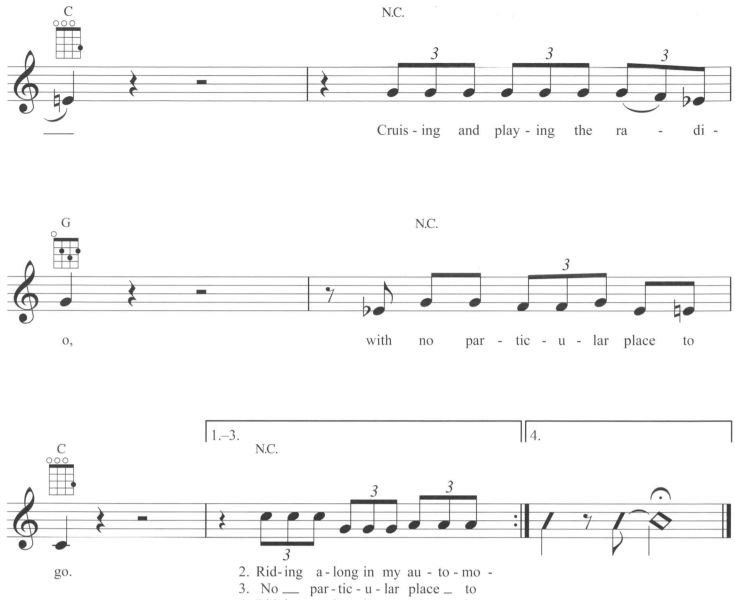

Cruis - ing   and   play - ing   the   ra   -   di -

o,   with   no   par - tic - u - lar   place   to

1.–3.   **4.**

go.   2. Rid-ing   a - long in   my au - to - mo -
                             3. No __ par - tic - u - lar place __ to
                             4. Rid-ing   a - long in   my cal - a - boose, __

Additional Lyrics

2. Riding along in my automobile,
   I was anxious to tell her the way I feel.
   So I told her softly and sincere,
   And she leaned and whispered in my ear,
   Cuddlin' more and driving slow,
   With no particular place to go.

3. No particular place to go,
   So we parked way out on the cocamo.
   The night was young and the moon was gold,
   So we both decided to take a stroll.
   Can you imagine the way I felt?
   I couldn't unfasten her safety belt.

4. Riding along in my calaboose,
   Still trying to get her belt a-loose.
   All the way home I held a grudge
   For the safety belt that wouldn't budge.
   Cruising and playing the radio,
   With no particular place to go.

Old Time Rock & Roll

Words and Music by George Jackson and Thomas E. Jones III

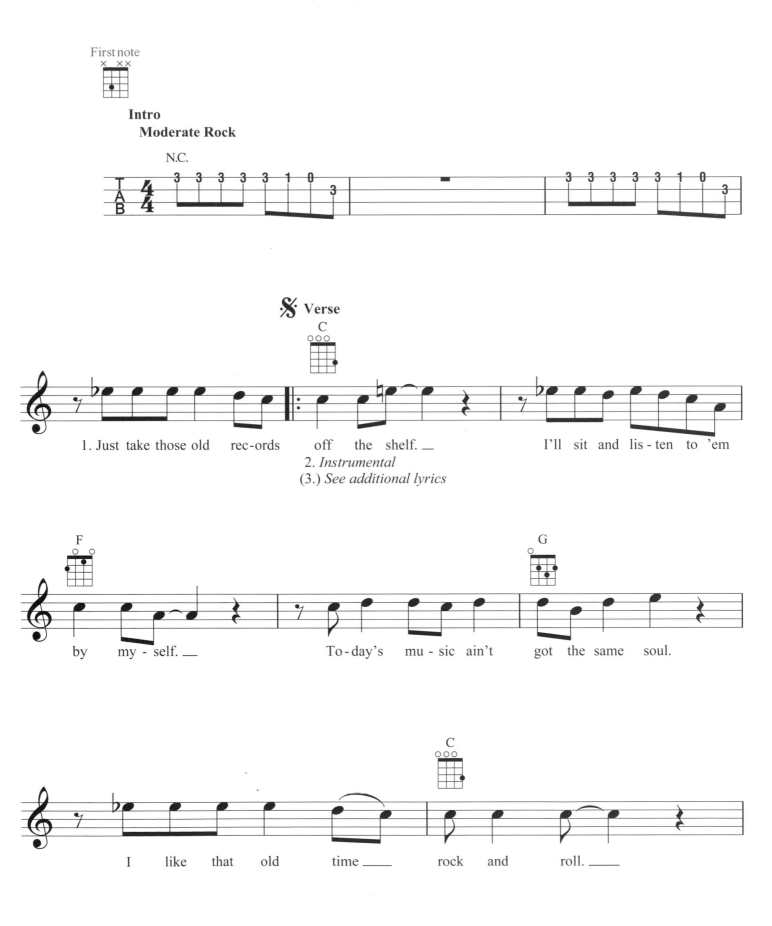

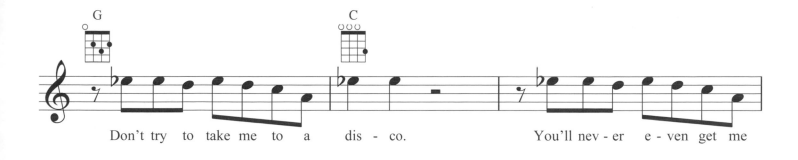

Don't try to take me to a dis - co. You'll nev - er e - ven get me

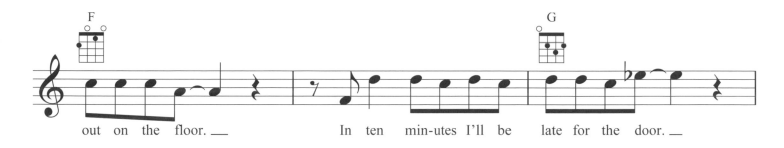

out on the floor. ___ In ten min-utes I'll be late for the door. ___

To Coda

I like that old time ___ rock and roll. ___ Still like that old time ___

Chorus

rock and roll. ___ That kind of mu - sic just soothes the soul. ___

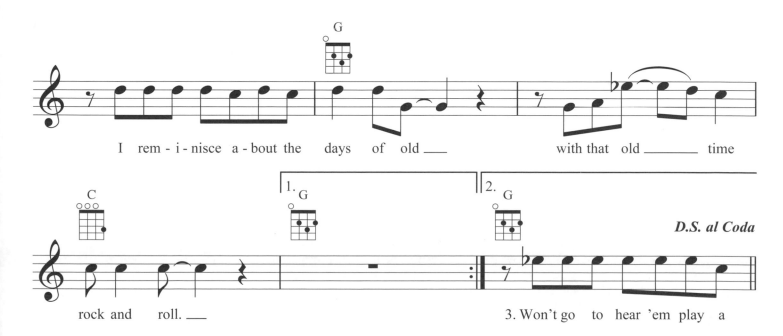

I rem - i - nisce a - bout the days of old ___ with that old ___ time

D.S. al Coda

rock and roll. ___ 3. Won't go to hear 'em play a

Additional Lyrics

3. Won't go to hear 'em play a tango.
   I'd rather hear some blues or funky old soul.
   There's only one sure way to get me to go:
   Start playin' old time rock and roll.
   Call me a relic, call me what you will.
   Say I'm old-fashioned, say I'm over the hill.
   Today's music ain't got the same soul.
   I like that old time rock and roll.

Mustang Sally

Words and Music by Bonny Rice

Oh, I guess I'll have to put your flat feet on the ground.

Chorus

All you wan-na do is ride _____ a-round, Sal-ly. (Ride, Sal-ly, ride.) _____

All you wan-na do is ride _____ a-round, Sal-ly. (Ride, Sal-ly, ride.) _

_____ All you wan-na do is ride _____ a-round, Sal-ly.

(Ride, Sal-ly, ride.) _____ All you wan-na do is ride _

Rain

Words and Music by John Lennon and Paul McCartney

1. If the rain comes, they run and hide their heads.
(2.) sun shines, they they slip in-to the shade

They might as well be dead if the rain comes,
and sip their lem-on-ade when the sun shines,

if the rain comes.
when the sun shines.

1. comes.   2. When the shines.

Chorus

Rain,

I don't mind. ___

Shine, ___

the weath-er's fine. ___

3. I can
4. Can you

Verse

show you that when it starts to rain,
hear me, that when it rains and shines, it's

ev-'ry-thing's the same. I can show you.
just a state of mind? Can you hear me?

I can show you.
Can you hear me?

Ring of Fire

Words and Music by Merle Kilgore and June Carter

1. Love is a burn - ing thing,
(2.) *See additional lyrics*

and it makes

a fier - y ring.

Bound by wild __ de - sire, __

I fell in - to a

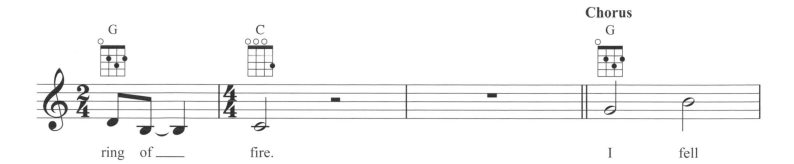

ring   of ___   fire.   I   fell

in - to   a   burn-in'   ring   of   fi - re.   I   went

down,   down,   down,   and the   flames   went   high- er.   And it

burns,   burns,   burns,   the   ring ___   of   fi - re,

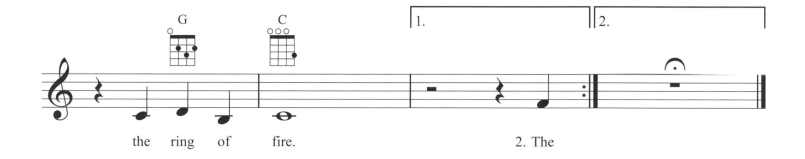

the   ring   of   fire.   2. The

Additional Lyrics

2. The taste of love is sweet
   When hearts like ours meet.
   I fell for you like a child,
   Oh, but the fire went wild.

Rock Around the Clock

Words and Music by Max C. Freedman and Jimmy DeKnight

Chorus

rock a - round the clock to - night, __ we're gon - na rock, rock, rock, 'til

broad day - light. __ We're gon - na rock, gon - na rock a - round __ the clock __ to - night. __

1.–5.

6.

2., 4., 6. When the __ (Instrumental)
5. When it's

Additional Lyrics

2. When the clock strikes two, and three and four,
   If the band slows down we'll yell for more.

4. When the chimes ring five and six and seven,
   We'll be rockin' up in seventh heav'n.

5. When it's eight, nine, ten, eleven, too,
   I'll be goin' strong and so will you.

6. When the clock strikes twelve, we'll cool off, then,
   Start a rockin' 'round the clock again.

Rock This Town

Words and Music by Brian Setzer

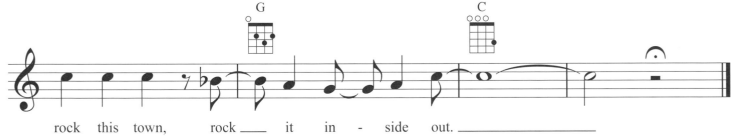

Additional Lyrics

2. Well, we found a little place that really didn't look half bad.
   I had a whiskey on the rocks and change of a dollar for the jukebox.
   Well, I put a quarter right into that can,
   But all it played was disco, man!
   Come on, baby, baby, let's get outta here right away.

3. Well, we're havin' a ball just a-boppin' on the big dance floor.
   Well, there's a real square cat, he looks a-nineteen seventy-four.
   Well, he looked at me once, he looked at me twice.
   He looked at me again and there's a-gonna be a fight!
   We're gonna rock this town, we're gonna rip this place apart.

Ready Teddy

Words and Music by John Marascalco and Robert Blackwell

Rockin' Robin

Words and Music by J. Thomas

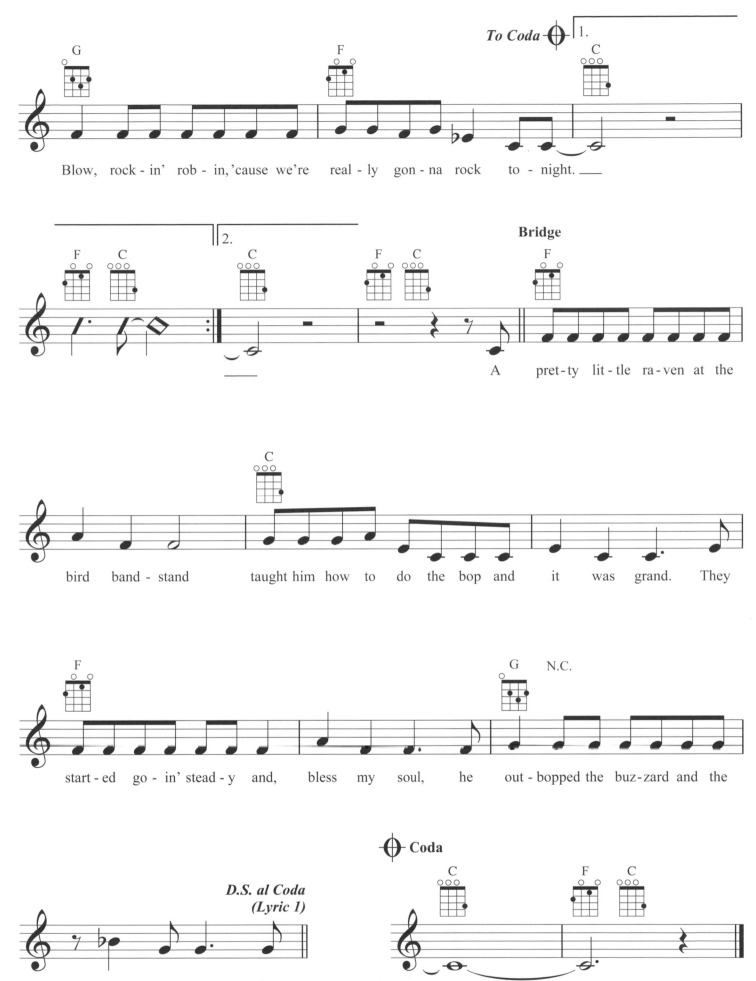

Sad Songs
(Say So Much)

Words and Music by Elton John and Bernie Taupin

1. Guess there are times when we all need to share a little pain and iron-ing out the rough spots is the hard-est part when mem-o-ries re-main.

(2.) suf-fer-in' e-nough, oh, to write it down when ev-'ry sin-gle word makes sense, then it's eas-i-er to have those songs a-round.

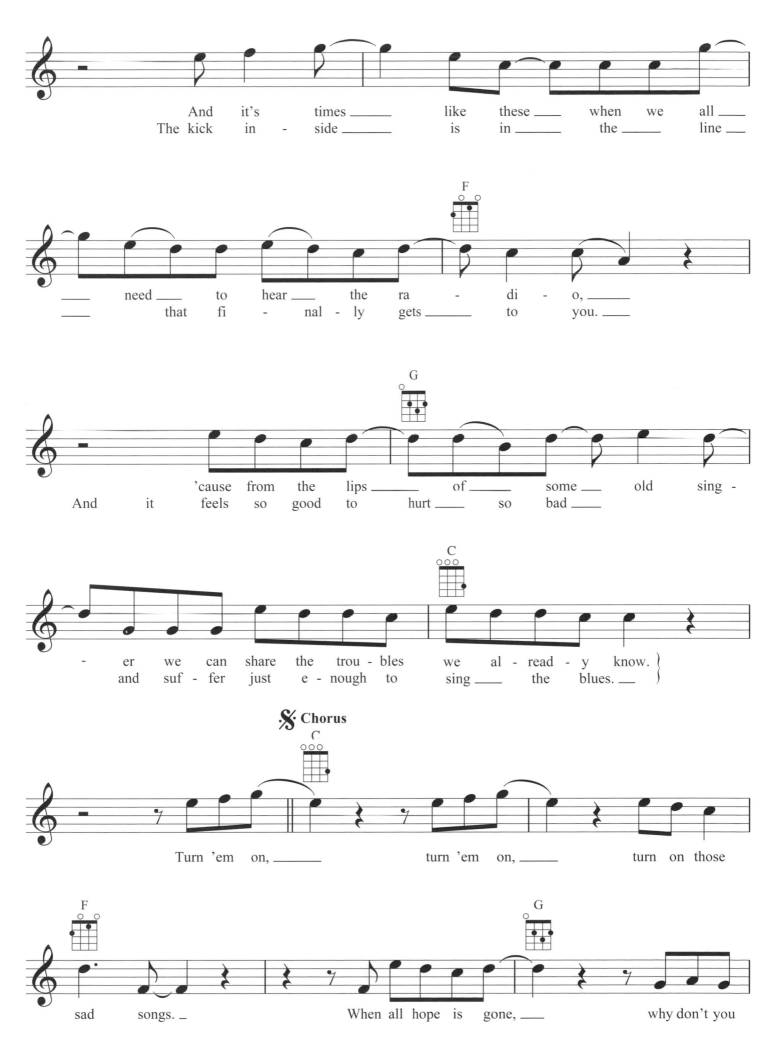

And it's times ___ like these ___ when we all ___
The kick in - side ___ is in ___ the ___ line ___

___ need ___ to hear ___ the ra - di - o, ___
___ that fi - nal - ly gets ___ to you. ___

And it 'cause from the lips ___ of ___ some ___ old sing -
it feels so good to hurt ___ so bad ___

- er we can share the trou - bles we al - read - y know.
and suf - fer just e - nough to sing ___ the blues. ___

Chorus

Turn 'em on, ___ turn 'em on, ___ turn on those

sad songs. ___ When all hope is gone, ___ why don't you

To Coda ⊕

Bridge

See You Later, Alligator

Words and Music by Robert Guidry

Additional Lyrics

3. She said, "I'm sorry, pretty daddy, you know my love is just for you."
   She said, "I'm sorry, pretty daddy, you know my love is just for you.
   Won't you say that you'll forgive me, and say your love for me is true?"

4. I said, "Wait a minute, 'gator, I know you meant it just for play."
   I said, "Wait a minute, 'gator, I know you meant it just for play.
   Don't you know you really hurt me, and this is what I have to say:

Shelter from the Storm

Words and Music by Bob Dylan

First note

Verse
Moderately, in 2

1. 'Twas in an-oth-er life-time, one of toil and
2.–10. *See additional lyrics*

blood, when black-ness was a vir-tue and the road was full of mud. _

___ I came in from the wil-der-ness, ___ a

crea-ture void ___ of form. ___ "Come in," she said, "I'll give ya

shel-ter from ___ the storm."

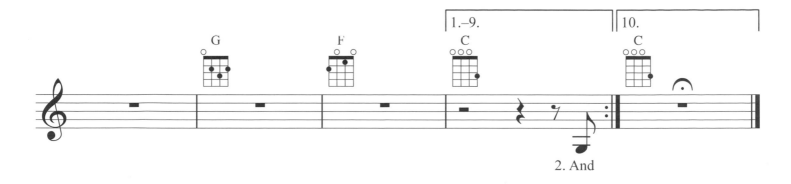

Additional Lyrics

2. And if I pass this way again, you can rest assured
   I'll always do my best for her; on that I give my word.
   In a world of steel-eyed death and men who are fighting to be warm,
   "Come in," she said, "I'll give ya shelter from the storm."

3. Not a word was spoke between us; there was little risk involved.
   Everything up to that point had been left unresolved.
   Try imagining a place where it's always safe and warm.
   "Come in," she said, "I'll give ya shelter from the storm."

4. I was burned out from exhaustion, buried in the hail,
   Poisoned in the bushes and blown out on the trail,
   Hunted like a crocodile, ravaged in the corn.
   "Come in," she said, "I'll give ya shelter from the storm."

5. Suddenly, I turned around and she was standin' there
   With silver bracelets on her wrists and flowers in her hair.
   She walked up to me so gracefully and took my crown of thorns.
   "Come in," she said, "I'll give ya shelter from the storm."

6. Now there's a wall between us; somethin' there's been lost.
   I took too much for granted; I got my signals crossed.
   Just to think that it all began on a non-eventful morn.
   "Come in," she said, "I'll give ya shelter from the storm."

7. Well, the deputy walks on hard nails and the preacher rides a mount,
   But nothing really matters much; it's doom alone that counts.
   And the one-eyed undertaker, he blows a futile horn.
   "Come in," she said, "I'll give ya shelter from the storm."

8. I've heard newborn babies wailin' like a mournin' dove
   And old men with broken teeth stranded without love.
   Do I understand your question, man? Is it hopeless and forlorn?
   "Come in," she said, "I'll give ya shelter from the storm."

9. In a little hilltop village, they gambled for my clothes.
   I bargained for salvation and she gave me a lethal dose.
   I offered up my innocence; I got repaid with scorn.
   "Come in," she said, "I'll give ya shelter from the storm."

10. Well, I'm livin' in a foreign country, but I'm bound to cross the line.
    Beauty walks a razor's edge; someday I'll make it mine.
    If I could only turn back the clock to when God and her were born.
    "Come in," she said, "I'll give ya shelter from the storm."

Singing the Blues

Words and Music by Melvin Endsley

Spanish Harlem

Words and Music by Jerry Leiber and Phil Spector

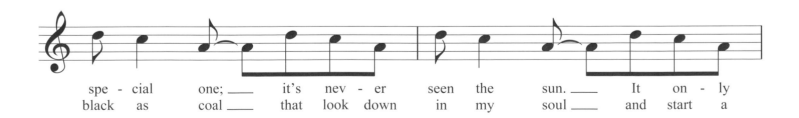

1., 2. There is a rose in Span - ish Har - lem,

a red rose up in Span - ish

Har - lem.

It is a
With eyes as

spe - cial one; ___ it's nev - er seen the sun. ___ It on - ly
black as coal ___ that look down in my soul ___ and start a

comes out when the moon is on the run and all the stars are gleam - ing. _____
fire ____ there, and then I lose con - trol. I have to beg your par - don. _____

____

It's grow - ing in the street, ___ right up
I'm going to pick that rose ___ and watch

1.

through the con - crete, but soft and sweet ___ and dream - ing. _____

2.

____   her as she grows

in my gar - den. _____

Sugar, Sugar

Words and Music by Andy Kim and Jeff Barry

you are my can - dy girl _____

and you've got me want - ing you. _____

Fine

Verse

1. I just can't be - lieve the love - li - ness of lov - ing you.
2. When I kissed you, girl, I knew _____ how sweet a kiss could be. (I

(I just can't be - lieve it's true.) _____
know how sweet a kiss can be.) _____

I just can't be - lieve the won - der of this feel - ing, too.
Like the sum - mer sun - shine, pour _____ your sweet - ness o - ver me.

1.

(I just can't be - lieve it's true.) _____ Ah!

Ruby Baby

Words and Music by Jerry Leiber and Mike Stoller

Ru - by, Ru - by, Ru - by, will you be mine?
Ru - by, Ru - by, Ru - by, will you be mine?

𝄋 Chorus

(Ru - by, Ru - by, Ru - by, ba - by.

Ru - by, Ru - by, Ru - by, ba - by. Ru - by, Ru - by,

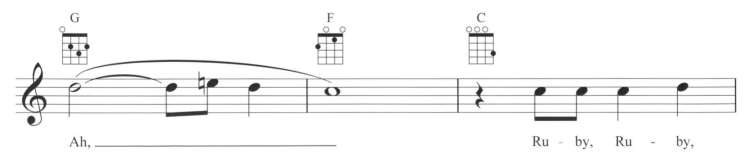

Ru - by, ba - by. Ru - by, Ru - by, Ru - by, ba - by.

Ah, _____ Ru - by, Ru - by,

To Coda ⊕   **Verse**

Ru - by, ba - by.)   3. I love this girl; I said - a Ru - by is her name. __

When this girl looks at me, she just

sets my soul a - flame. ___ Whoa, _____

___ got some hugs and - a kiss - es too, yeah, and I'm gon - na give them - a

all to you. Now lis - ten: Ru - by, Ru - by, when will you be

mine?

D.S. al Coda

Coda
Outro

Ru - by, Ru - by,

when will you be mine? _____

(Let Me Be Your)
Teddy Bear

Words and Music by Kal Mann and Bernie Lowe

rough. I don't wan-na be a li - on, 'cause

li - ons ain't the kind ___ you love e - nough.

%. Verse

N.C.

2. I just a-wan-na (4.) be your ___ ted-dy bear. ___

___ Put a chain a-

To Coda ⊕

round my neck, ___ and lead me an-y-where. ___ Oh, let me

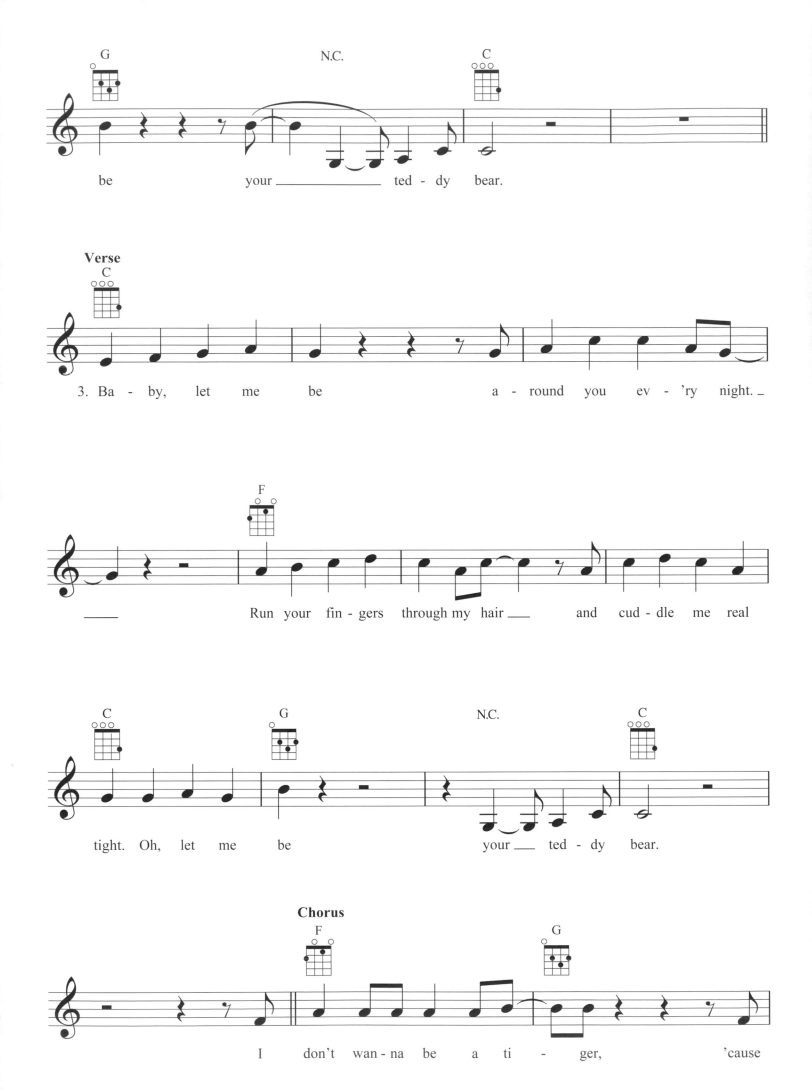

Too Much

Words and Music by Lee Rosenberg and Bernard Weinman

Twist and Shout

Words and Music by Bert Russell and Phil Medley

You know you look so good. (Look so good.) You know you got me
You know you twist so fine. (Twist so fine.) Come on and twist a lit - tle

go - in' now, (Got me goin'.) ___ just like I knew ___ you would. ___
clos - er now, (Twist a lit - tle clos - er.) and let me know ___ that you're

To Coda ⊕

1.

2.

___ (Like I knew you would.) Well, shake it up, ba -
mine. (Let me know you're mine.) Ooh. ___

Interlude

Play 4 times

Ah. Ah.

D.S. al Coda

Ah. Ah. Ah. ___ Shake it up, ba -

Walk of Life

Words and Music by Mark Knopfler

1., 3. Here comes John - ny sing - ing old - ies, gold - ies,
2. *See additional lyrics*

be - bop - a - lu - la, ba - by, what I say.

Here comes John - ny sing - ing, "I Got a Wom - an,"

down in the tun - nels tryin' to make it pay.

Chorus

1. He got the ac - tion, he got the mo - tion. Oh yeah, _ the
2., 3. *See additional lyrics*

boy can play. Ded - i - ca - tion, __ de - vo - tion,

turn - ing all the night - time in - to the day. __ He do the

song a - bout the sweet lov - in' wom - an, he do the song a - bout the knife.

Then he do the walk, he do the walk of

life. Yeah, __ he do the walk of life. _____

Interlude

(Instrumental)

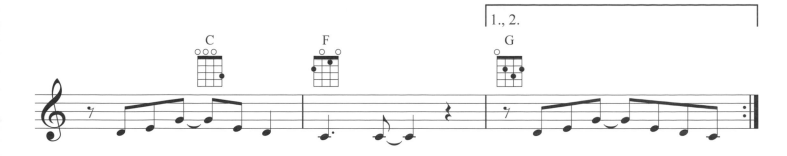

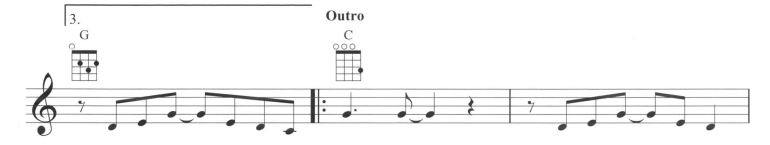

Additional Lyrics

2. Here comes Johnny, gonna tell you the story;
   Hand me down my walkin' shoes.
   Here comes Johnny with the power and the glory,
   Back-beat the talkin' blues.

Chorus 2: He got the action, he got the motion.
   Oh yeah, the boy can play.
   Dedication, devotion,
   Turning all the nighttime into the day.
   He do the song about the sweet lovin' woman,
   He do the song about the knife.
   Then he do the walk, he do the walk of life.
   Yeah, he do the walk of life.

Chorus 3: He got the action, he got the motion.
   Yeah, the boy can play.
   Dedication, devotion,
   Turning all the nighttime into the day.
   And after all the violence and double talk,
   There's just a song in all the trouble and the strife.
   You do the walk, you do the walk of life.
   Mmm, you do the walk of life.

Up Around the Bend

Words and Music by John Fogerty

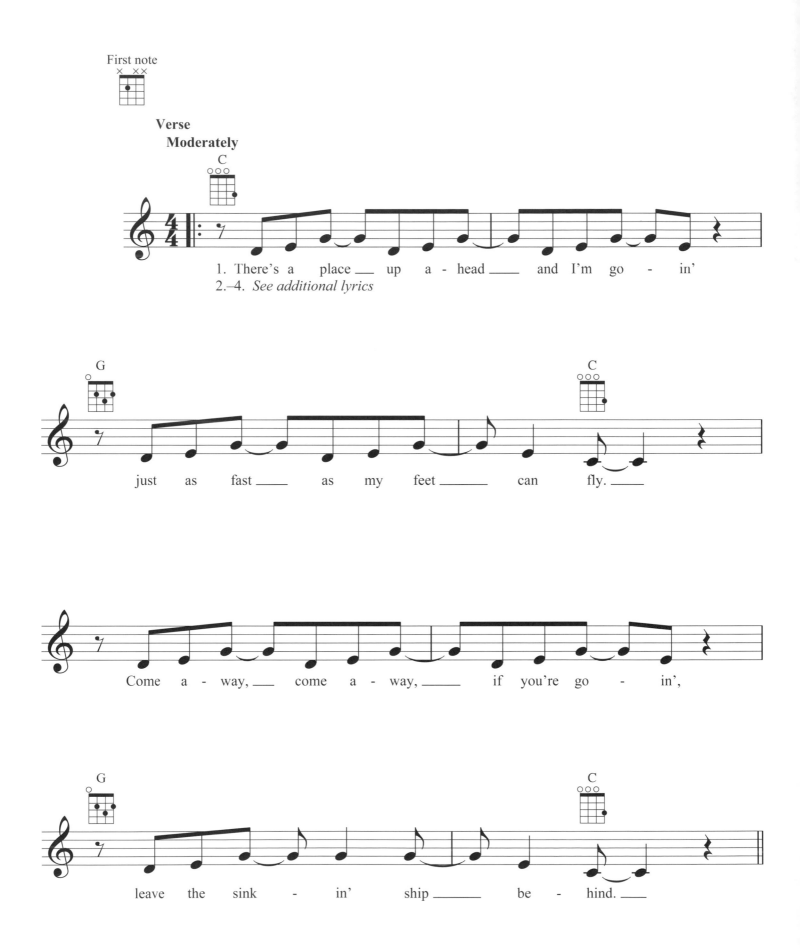

1. There's a place ___ up a - head ___ and I'm go - in'
2.–4. *See additional lyrics*

just as fast ___ as my feet ___ can fly. ___

Come a - way, ___ come a - way, ___ if you're go - in',

leave the sink - in' ship ___ be - hind. ___

Additional Lyrics

2. Bring a song and a smile for the banjo.
   Better get while the gettin's good.
   Hitch a ride to end of the highway
   Where the neons turn to wood.

3. You can ponder perpetual motion,
   Fix your mind on a crystal day.
   Always time for a good conversation,
   There's an ear for what you say.

4. Catch a ride to the end of the highway
   And we'll meet by the big red tree.
   There's a place up ahead and I'm goin'.
   Come along, come along with me.

Used to Love Her

Words and Music by W. Axl Rose, Slash, Izzy Stradlin',
Duff McKagan and Steven Adler

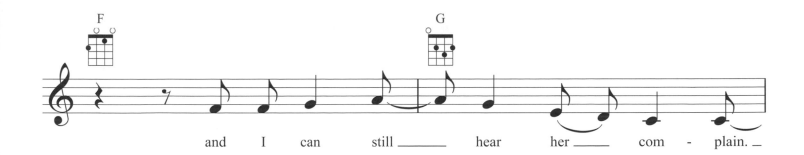

and I can still ____ hear her ____ com - plain. ____

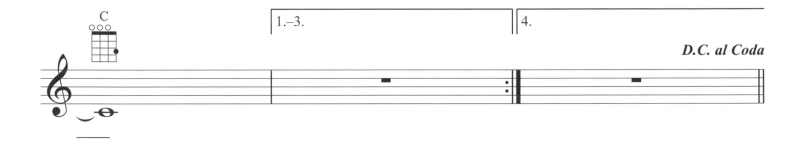

D.C. al Coda

1.–3.　　　　　4.

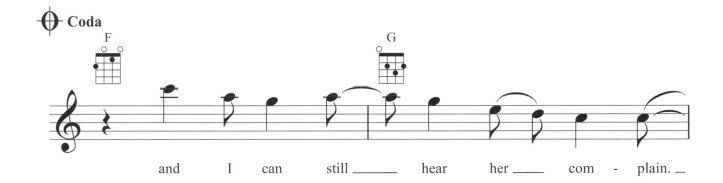

Coda

and I can still ____ hear her ____ com - plain. ____

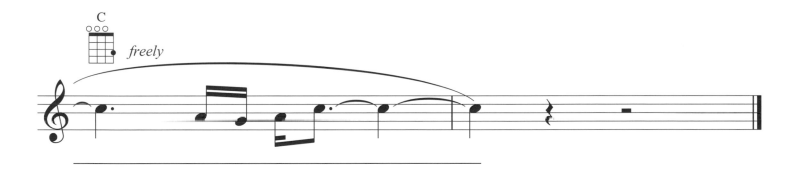

freely

Additional Lyrics

2. I used to love her, but I had to kill her.
   I used to love her, but I had to kill her.
   I knew I'd miss her, so I had to keep her.
   She's buried right in my back yard.

3. I used to love her, but I had to kill her.
   I used to love her, but I had to kill her.
   She bitched so much she drove me nuts,
   And now we're happier this way.

Yakety Yak

Words and Music by Jerry Leiber and Mike Stoller

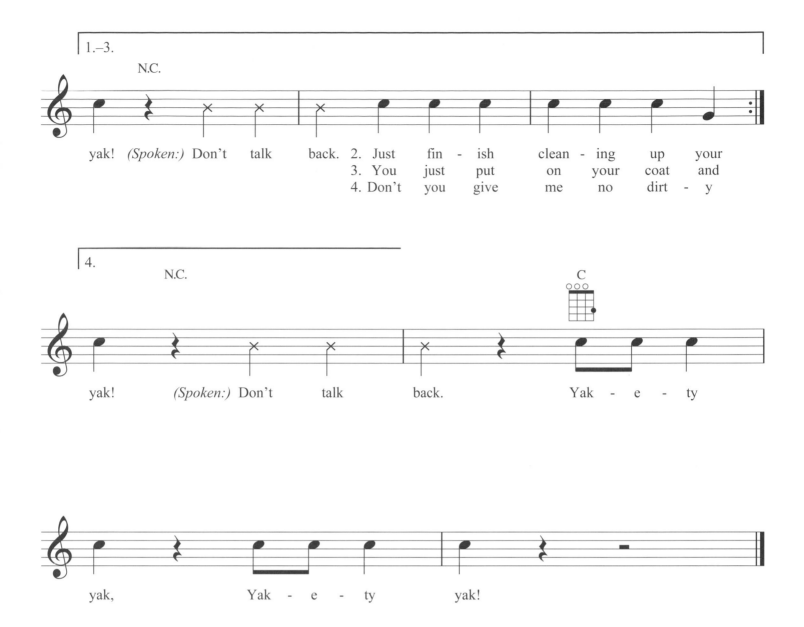

Additional Lyrics

2. Just finish cleaning up your room.
   Let's see that dust fly with that broom.
   Get all that garbage out of sight,
   Or you don't go out Friday night.
   Yakety yak! *(Spoken:) Don't talk back.*

3. You just put on your coat and hat
   And walk yourself to the laundrymat.
   And when you finish doing that,
   Bring in the dog and put out the cat.
   Yakety yak! *(Spoken:) Don't talk back.*

4. Don't you give me no dirty looks.
   Your father's hip; he knows what cooks.
   Just tell your hoodlum friend outside,
   You ain't got time to take a ride.
   Yakety yak! *(Spoken:) Don't talk back.*

Time for Me to Fly

Words and Music by Kevin Cronin

Chorus

steal - in' your love _____ a - way 'cause you nev - er give _____
nough of the false - ness of a worn - out re - la -

_____ it; peel - in' the years _____ a - way, and
- tion e - nough of the jeal - ous - y and the

we can't re - live _____ it. }
in - tol - er - a - tion. }
I make you laugh, _

_____ and _ you make me cry. _____

I be - lieve it's time _____ for me _ to fly. _____

1.

UKULELE CHORD SONGBOOKS

This series features convenient 6" x 9" books with complete lyrics and chord symbols for dozens of great songs. Each song also includes chord grids at the top of every page and the first notes of the melody for easy reference.

ACOUSTIC ROCK

60 tunes: American Pie • Band on the Run • Catch the Wind • Daydream • Every Rose Has Its Thorn • Hallelujah • Iris • More Than Words • Patience • The Sound of Silence • Space Oddity • Sweet Talkin' Woman • Wake up Little Susie • Who'll Stop the Rain • and more.
00702482 . . . .$15.99

THE BEATLES

100 favorites: Across the Universe • Carry That Weight • Dear Prudence • Good Day Sunshine • Here Comes the Sun • If I Fell • Love Me Do • Michelle • Ob-La-Di, Ob-La-Da • Revolution • Something • Ticket to Ride • We Can Work It Out • and many more.
00703065 . . . . $19.99

BEST SONGS EVER

70 songs: All I Ask of You • Bewitched • Edelweiss • Just the Way You Are • Let It Be • Memory • Moon River • Over the Rainbow • Someone to Watch over Me • Unchained Melody • You Are the Sunshine of My Life • You Raise Me Up • and more.
00117050 . . . .$16.99

CHILDREN'S SONGS

80 classics: Alphabet Song • "C" Is for Cookie • Do-Re-Mi • I'm Popeye the Sailor Man • Mickey Mouse March • Oh! Susanna • Polly Wolly Doodle • Puff the Magic Dragon • The Rainbow Connection • Sing • Three Little Fishies (Itty Bitty Poo) • and many more.
00702473 . . . .$14.99

CHRISTMAS CAROLS

75 favorites: Away in a Manger • Coventry Carol • The First Noel • Good King Wenceslas • Hark! the Herald Angels Sing • I Saw Three Ships • Joy to the World • O Little Town of Bethlehem • Still, Still, Still • Up on the Housetop • What Child Is This? • and more.
00702474 . . . .$14.99

CHRISTMAS SONGS

55 Christmas classics: Do They Know It's Christmas? • Frosty the Snow Man • Happy Xmas (War Is Over) • Jingle-Bell Rock • Little Saint Nick • The Most Wonderful Time of the Year • White Christmas • and more.
00101776 . . . .$14.99

ISLAND SONGS

60 beach party tunes: Blue Hawaii • Day-O (The Banana Boat Song) • Don't Worry, Be Happy • Island Girl • Kokomo • Lovely Hula Girl • Mele Kalikimaka • Red, Red Wine • Surfer Girl • Tiny Bubbles • Ukulele Lady • and many more.
00702471 . . . .$16.99

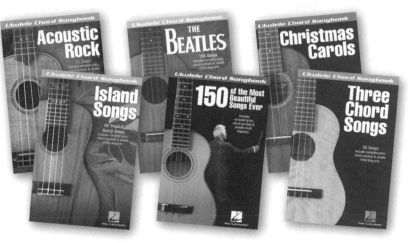

150 OF THE MOST BEAUTIFUL SONGS EVER

150 melodies: Always • Bewitched • Candle in the Wind • Endless Love • In the Still of the Night • Just the Way You Are • Memory • The Nearness of You • People • The Rainbow Connection • Smile • Unchained Melody • What a Wonderful World • Yesterday • and more.
00117051 . . . .$24.99

PETER, PAUL & MARY

Over 40 songs: And When I Die • Blowin' in the Wind • Goodnight, Irene • If I Had a Hammer (The Hammer Song) • Leaving on a Jet Plane • Puff the Magic Dragon • This Land Is Your Land • We Shall Overcome • Where Have All the Flowers Gone? • and more.
00121822 . . . .$12.99

THREE CHORD SONGS

60 songs: Bad Case of Loving You • Bang a Gong (Get It On) • Blue Suede Shoes • Cecilia • Get Back • Hound Dog • Kiss • Me and Bobby McGee • Not Fade Away • Rock This Town • Sweet Home Chicago • Twist and Shout • You Are My Sunshine • and more.
00702483 . . . .$14.99

TOP HITS

31 hits: The A Team • Born This Way • Forget You • Ho Hey • Jar of Hearts • Little Talks • Need You Now • Rolling in the Deep • Teenage Dream • Titanium • We Are Never Ever Getting Back Together • and more.
00115929 . . . .$14.99

Prices, contents, and availability subject to change without notice.

Learn to play the
Ukulele
with these great Hal Leonard books!

Hal Leonard Ukulele Method

Book 1
by Lil' Rev

The *Hal Leonard Ukulele Method* is designed for anyone just learning to play ukulele. This comprehensive and easy-to-use beginner's guide by acclaimed performer and uke master Lil' Rev includes many fun songs of different styles to learn and play. The accompanying audio contains 46 tracks of songs for demonstration and play along. Includes: types of ukuleles, tuning, music reading, melody playing, chords, strumming, scales, tremolo, music notation and tablature, a variety of music styles, ukulele history and much more.

00695847 Book Only	$6.99
00695832 Book/Online Audio	$10.99
00320534 DVD	$14.95

Book 2

00695948 Book Only	$6.99
00695949 Book/Online Audio	$10.99

Ukulele Chord Finder

00695803 9" x 12"	$7.99
00695902 6" x 9"	$6.99
00696472 Book 1 with Online Audio + Chord Finder	$15.99

Ukulele Scale Finder

00696378 9" x 12"	$6.99

Easy Songs for Ukulele

00695904 Book/Online Audio	$14.99
00695905 Book	$7.99

Ukulele for Kids

00696468 Book/Online Audio	$12.99
00244855 Method & Songbook	$19.99

Baritone Ukulele Method – Book 1

00696564 Book/Online Audio	$10.99

Jake Shimabukuro Teaches Ukulele Lessons

Learn notes, chords, songs, and playing techniques from the master of modern ukulele! In this unique book with online video, Jake Shimabukuro will get you started on playing the ukulele. The book includes full transcriptions of every example, the video features Jake teaching you everything you need to know plus video of Jake playing all the examples.

00320992 Book/Online Video $19.99

Ukulele Aerobics

For All Levels, from Beginner to Advanced
by Chad Johnson

This package provides practice material for every day of the week and includes an online audio access code for all the workouts in the book. Techniques covered include: strumming, fingerstyle, slides, bending, damping, vibrato, tremolo and more.

00102162 Book/Online Audio $19.99

Fretboard Roadmaps – Ukulele

The Essential Patterns That All the Pros Know and Use

by Fred Sokolow & Jim Beloff

Take your uke playing to the next level! Tunes and exercises in standard notation and tab illustrate each technique. Absolute beginners can follow the diagrams and instruction step-by-step, while intermediate and advanced players can use the chapters non-sequentially to increase their understanding of the ukulele. The audio includes 59 demo and play-along tracks.

00695901 Book/Online Audio $14.99

All About Ukulele

A Fun and Simple Guide to Playing Ukulele

by Chad Johnson

If you wish there was a fun and engaging way to motivate you in your uke playing quest, then this is it: All About Ukulele is for you. Whether it's learning to read music, playing in a band, finding the right instrument, or all of the above, this enjoyable guide will help you.

00233655 Book/Online Audio $19.99

Play Ukulele Today!

A Complete Guide to the Basics
by Barrett Tagliarino

This is the ultimate self-teaching method for ukulele! Includes audio with full demo tracks and over 60 great songs. You'll learn: care for the instrument; how to produce sound; reading music notation and rhythms; and more.

00699638 Book/Online Audio	$10.99
00293927 Book 1 & 2/Online Media	$19.99

HAL•LEONARD®
www.halleonard.com

HAL•LEONARD® UKULELE PLAY-ALONG

AUDIO ACCESS INCLUDED

Now you can play your favorite songs on your uke with great-sounding backing tracks to help you sound like a bona fide pro! The audio also features playback tools so you can adjust the tempo without changing the pitch and loop challenging parts.

Prices, contents, and availability subject to change without notice.

HAL•LEONARD®

www.halleonard.com

0719
483